Just Winging It

Prayers for My Pilot

Angelia J Griffin

Just Winging It: Prayers for My Pilot

Published by AGF Publishing
PO BOX 7023
Cut and Shoot, TX 77303 USA
www.agfpublishing.com

ISBN: 978-1-4951-8864-0 (paperback)
LCCN: 2017913168

To Kevin who always encourages me to F.L.Y.

Just Winging It:

Prayers for My Pilot
Prayers for My Pilot Wife

Table of Contents

Preflight Check

AVIATION MARRIAGE IS A UNIQUE and beautiful entity. Your husband is not an inconvenience or a blight on the flight plans of your life. He is a beautiful gift, a co-pilot with whom to share the laughter and tears that the journey inevitably brings. He is the man you vowed to spend forever with, to love and to cherish. The world would have us throw up our hands in defeat and hit the eject button as soon as the going gets a little turbulent. I say let's lock hands in defiance to the world and pronounce at the top of our lungs, "My husband is worth fighting for!"

Life with a traveling spouse certainly comes with its own unique set of hurdles. There are many days of blue skies and smooth flying, but there are also those filled with headwinds and turbulence. An aviation marriage is like a rare, beautiful plane. You don't scrap the entire aircraft because of a broken rivet. The plane is much too precious. Instead, you fix the rivet.

Life's storms are sometimes unavoidable. When the winds buffet you and the darkness closes in, grip the yoke with all your might, contact the control tower for directions, and hold on tight for the ride. There is incredible beauty on the other side of the storm. Believe me, I've seen it.

For even more encouragement, support, and useful tips on loving your aviation spouse well, please join me on my website at thepilotwifelife.com or my Facebook page at @thepilotwifelife. I can't wait to embark upon this journey with you!

Cleared for Takeoff

IT IS IMPOSSIBLE TO HATE someone for whom we are earnestly praying. It keeps our hearts humble and reminds us that our spouses deserve the same amazing grace that God has given to us. It helps us to revel in our blessings instead of focusing on the things we do not have. It teaches us to love fiercely, speak gently, and act honorably toward our spouse and God. We are all flawed and imperfect, but love covers a multitude of sins. Prayer is the channel through which love flows.

Aviation life is unpredictable, chaotic, and busy…and that's on the easy days! For this reason, there is no specific right or wrong way to work your way through this book. It's a guilt free journey!

It was purposely written to be used in whatever manner works best for you and your life situation. There are 31 prayers so that those of you who are the scheduled type have a full month of daily prayers. However, if you can only find time to sit down every other day, or if you miss a day or six when the pilot is home (or he's gone and the kids are sick with the plague…again), it's okay! There's no timeframe; simply pick it back up when you are able.

It also does not have to be read in any particular order. If you are a front-to-back reader, great! If there is a specific hurdle you are facing, peruse the table of contents and skip right to that prayer. If you need to pray the same prayer over and over, for days or even weeks, do it! If you want to pray multiple prayers in one day, go for it!

This book was written as a pliable resource to help guide you in your aviation prayer life. Use it the way that best suits your needs, but *use* it! I do encourage you to pray these prayers (or your own) as often as possible because the more regularly you pray, the quicker and deeper it will begin to work in your marriage.

I have also included a handy area before each section so that you can add your own notes, thoughts, and prayers as you go. I highly suggest keeping a journal as you work through this book. A prayer journal is a great way to look back over time and see how God has moved in your marriage!

Prayer is a powerful tool in your marriage. Whether your marriage is already soaring and you want to keep it that way or you are struggling and long to experience the joy of marriage as it was meant to be, this book is going to be a precious resource. I believe you are going to be amazed by the positive changes in your heart and marriage as you learn to make specific, intentional prayer for your husband a regular habit.

Before you start your new prayer journey, let your pilot know you are praying for him. Turn to page 136 of this book and remove the prayer card you find there. Be sure to sign it and place it somewhere where your husband will find it while he is away on his next trip. Oh, and if you just so happen to tuck one of his favorite treats into his bag alongside it, I'm *sure* he won't mind.

I *love* you, ladies. May your marriages be filled with blue skies and tailwinds.

~Angelia (a fellow pilot wife)

MY
PRAYER
FOR
YOU

Proverb 31

Dear Heavenly Father,

THANK YOU FOR THE BEAUTIFUL woman reading this book. Thank you for her willingness to embark upon this prayer journey in order to strengthen her aviation marriage. I pray that you would soften her heart toward her husband and bless her with clarity and perspective. Fill her with a fierce love for you and for her spouse as she undertakes this journey. I pray you bless her with patience for your work in her marriage, endurance through the trials, and gentleness in her words. May her heart and marriage be transformed from the inside out, and may she experience the overwhelming joy of marriage as you created it to be. Press into her husband, Lord. Let his heart also be transformed. Create in him the faithful, adoring, gentle husband that she deserves and you desire for him to be. Teach them to love each other well, leaning not on their own finite abilities to forgive, change, and grow, but rather on your infinite power and overwhelming grace. Open their hearts, Lord, and give them an aviation marriage transformed.

Amen

CLARITY
(MINE)

1 Corinthians 13:12

Notes

Dear Heavenly Father,

THANK YOU FOR MY PILOT. Thank you for blessing me with a talented, passionate, hardworking man to share this life with. I know that he is a good man, Lord, but sometimes life as a pilot's wife can be lonely and hard. Sometimes my long-term perspective of my pilot becomes blurred by the day-to-day turbulence of this lifestyle. Help me see my husband clearly, perhaps even for the very first time. Open my eyes, Lord, so that I might truly see his heart. Help me to view this life from his perspective. Help me to deeply understand my pilot and the loneliness, stresses, and temptations that he faces on a daily basis. Help me cherish my spouse and love him unapologetically. Teach me to love him in the ways he needs to be loved and see him not through my human eyes but through your perfect eyes of grace. He's more than a pilot, or a husband, or a father - he is your son, created in your image and unconditionally loved by you. Give me a heart of compassion and a deep, unwavering love for my husband. Forgive me for the times when I have allowed my pride to blind me to his needs and his perspective. Show me how to pray for my pilot, intentionally, sincerely, daily. Lord, help me to love him well and to be the wife he needs and deserves.

Amen

CLARITY
(HIS)

Ephesians 5:25

Notes

Dear Heavenly Father,

MY PILOT IS AN AMAZING man. He is my husband, my lover, my confidante, my best friend. He is a good man who strives to provide for me and love me the best he knows how. Thank you, Lord, for allowing me to be his wife. He is a beautiful gift. However, sometimes I know it is hard for him to see the pilot wife lifestyle from my perspective, and he can become frustrated. I pray that you would help him see aviation life through my eyes. I want him to know that I love being a pilot's wife and wouldn't trade our life together for the world, but I also want him to understand the sacrifices and struggles that I willingly and lovingly endure to support his career. Give him compassion for my feelings and experiences. Help me to forgive him for the times when he sees me only through the cloudy lenses of selfish pride. Open the eyes of his heart, Lord. Reveal me to my pilot through your perfect, loving lenses. I am a complex, emotional, intricate woman with real emotional and physical needs. Teach him to love me in the ways that I need to feel loved. Give me the courage to tell him exactly what it is I really need. Reveal to him ways to show me the appreciation, affirmation, and love that I so desperately seek to receive from him. Help my husband see me with shining clarity and love me for who I am, because I am a good woman, beautifully and wonderfully created by the work of your hand.

Amen

CAREER

Colossians 3:23

Notes

Dear Heavenly Father,

MY HUSBAND IS AN INCREDIBLE, hardworking man. I am so grateful for his desire to provide for our family utilizing the passions and talents that you have placed into his heart. Thank you for the provision of the job that he has. I know that, though he loves to fly, he does not always enjoy the politics that accompany the profession. There are many obstacles and hurdles that he must navigate in his aviation career path, many of which I am unaware. I pray that he would be filled with deep satisfaction and experience great success in his career. I pray that he is surrounded by good, supportive people that make his job as enjoyable and as stress-free as possible. If he is currently seeking new employment or upgrade, I pray that you bless him with these things in a timely manner that will fill him with joy and contentment. During the stressful times of recurrent training, I pray you give him knowledge and peace of mind. Help him to be confident in himself and his abilities. As his wife, help me to be a great encourager on his career path. Do not let me be a constant headwind that makes his journey difficult, but rather give me the strength, courage, and wisdom to be the tailwinds that hasten him on his way.

Amen

ACCOUNTABILITY

Hebrews 3:13

Notes

Dear Heavenly Father,

I LOVE THE HUSBAND THAT you have chosen for me. I love the passion you have placed in his heart for his profession and his willingness to provide for us even though that means we are often apart. I know how incredibly difficult it must be for him on the road surrounded by constant temptations and lack of accountability. I pray that you would place Godly, trustworthy men in his life with whom he can speak candidly about the challenges of aviation life. Lord, I pray for accountability partners who are not afraid to speak truth in love to my pilot and who check on him and the status of his heart often. Provide mentors who support our marriage and pour positivity into him. Help my husband make choices that glorify you in all ways - mentally, physically, spiritually. Let him hide your word in his heart such that he is constantly convicted by your righteousness and draws on it in times of weakness. Create in me a wife in whom he can also confide in confidence and without fear of retribution. Encourage me to ask the difficult questions and listen to his answers with a gentle, compassionate heart. Help me be slow to speak and quick to listen. Lord, teach him to seek your will every single day. Keep his heart focused on the things that are pure and honorable and help him stay accountable to you and to our marriage.

Amen

SAFETY

Psalm 18:2

Notes

Dear Heavenly Father,

THANK YOU FOR PROVIDING MY husband with a career that satisfies his deepest passion for flight while at the same time allowing him to provide for our family. It fills my heart with great joy knowing that his lifelong dreams are being fulfilled every time he steps foot into the cockpit of his plane, and I get to be a part of that! Although his career is an amazing one, it also holds its share of dangers. Lord, I pray for my pilot's safety as he soars through the skies, travels down unknown roads in unfamiliar cities, and lays his head on a different hotel pillow each night. Place a hedge of protection around him as he travels. Allow no man of evil intent to encroach upon his zone of safety or to inflict harm upon him. Give knowledge, awareness, and foresight to the aviation mechanics, air traffic controllers, copilots, drivers on the roads, and all others who directly or inadvertently affect his safety and wellbeing. Continually hone my pilot's own skills, giving him the necessary composure and knowledge to operate the aircraft safely. My husband is one of my greatest treasures. Wherever he might be at this moment, surround him with your protection and guard him from all danger. Lord, I love my pilot fiercely, but I know you love him even more. I trust him into your capable hands. Let my prayers be the wings upon which he soars through this life. Watch over my husband as he travels, and bring him safely home to my eagerly awaiting arms.

Amen

RESPECT

1 Peter 2:17

Notes

Dear Heavenly Father,

MY HUSBAND IS A GREAT man with a good heart. He works hard, provides for our family, and tries his best to navigate his way through the flight paths of his career and life with integrity. I know that a wife's respect is very important to her husband. It's hard for me to fully understand, but respect is to the heart of a man as love is to the heart of a woman. I know that he needs to hear me verbalize that I am proud of him and that I respect him on a regular basis. He needs me to show him honor both publicly and privately. It is also important to my husband that I speak of him only in a respectful, honoring manner even when he is not present to hear as well as in all social media settings. A man who feels respected by his wife is a man who can conquer the world. He is also a man who would do anything for the woman he loves. Lord, help me to show my husband the respect he so deeply desires. Help me put aside my foolish pride and past hurts and tell my husband how proud I am of him. Fill my mouth with words that lift him up. Convict my heart and still my tongue before I speak any words that might purposefully or inadvertantly tear him down or hurt him. Give me a deep, rich understanding of my husband's needs as a man and show me how to fulfill them. Let him feel respected by me on a daily basis, never doubting my adoration and love for him.

Amen

LONELINESS

Genesis 2:18

Notes

Dear Heavenly Father,

LIFE ON THE ROAD IS incredibly lonely and difficult at times. The constantly fluctuating schedules, innumerable lonely nights, and missed special occasions are extremely hard on my pilot. I know that he often pretends to be strong because he doesn't want to burden me with his problems and because, quite frankly, that's what is expected of a man in our world. However, there is no community on the road, no familiarity, no comforts - just the endless march of unfamiliar faces, unfamiliar places, and unfamiliar spaces. I pray that my husband knows deep down in his heart that he is never forgotten. Help me to make him feel loved, even when he is far away from my arms. Drive back the loneliness that threatens to suffocate him and give him the strength he needs to face each day. Do not allow depression to have a stronghold in his heart, but rather constantly remind him that he is cherished and loved by you and by me, his wife. Sometimes I get so swamped at home holding down the fort and wallowing in my own daily grind that I forget that my guy has nothing but the stark walls of a hotel room to keep him company. He does not get to be greeted by the loving arms of his wife at the end of a hard day. Help me to be diligent about checking in on him while he is away, praying for him ceaselessly, encouraging him, and telling him how much I miss him so that he knows without a doubt that he is always right here in my heart. A loving, encouraging wife can make all the difference between a man who enjoys his career and one who resents it.

Amen

TEMPTATION
(HIS)

Matthew 26:41

Notes

Dear Heavenly Father,

MY HUSBAND IS AN INCREDIBLE pilot and an amazing husband. He is also a flesh-and-blood man with very real needs who spends far too many lonely nights on the road. Aviation is inarguably a career of opportunity. Everywhere he turns, he is surrounded by constant temptation with very few buffers. Lord, I pray that you shield his eyes and ears from the distracting noises of this world. Help him tune out the drone of worldliness that constantly bombards him. Encourage him to fill his body only with those things that keep him strong and healthy and to avoid foods and substances which are harmful. Guard his tongue and keep his conversations clean and appropriate, no matter who is listening or the company that he must keep. Let every word that falls from his lips and every action of his hand glorify you and honor me and convict him of any that do not. Do not let him fall victim to the very real lures of drunkenness, pornography, gossip, anger, discouragement, and discontentment. Temptation comes in a variety of guises. Lord, be his constant buffer and convict his heart with righteousness, giving him wisdom in discernment. Whatever is true, whatever is noble, whatever is right, whatever is pure, whatever is lovely, whatever is admirable - if anything is excellent or praiseworthy, let him think about such things.

Amen

TEMPTATION
(MINE)

Matthew 5:28

Notes

Dear Heavenly Father,

I AM SO GRATEFUL FOR the beautiful life you have chosen to give to me. I am truly a blessed woman. Thank you for the pilot that you created and chose to be my husband and soulmate. Each day as his wife is a precious gift from you. You know that sometimes life as a pilot's wife gets difficult, frustrating, and lonely and that sometimes distance can make the heart grow more distant. When he is gone and I am alone for long periods of time, it is easy for my heart to drift astray or grow weary. Guard my heart from all manner of temptation that comes my way. Do not let the distance become a steppingstone for temptation. Send me strong women of integrity to lift me up and speak loving truth into my life. Create within me a pure heart and a strong desire only for the man you chose for me. Lord, encourage me to take care of my body, filling it only with those things that make me strong and healthy and rejecting those that do not. Help me get plenty of rest and exercise even when life is chaotic and busy. Our actions and words reflect the overflow of our hearts. Protect my ears from words of negativity and gossip and fill my mouth and heart only with positive words that honor you and build up my spouse. Do not allow me to contemplate lies or manipulations for even a moment but instead give me a heart of wise discernment. Do not allow discontentment to have a foothold in my life, but rather place my focus on my abundant blessings. Guard my heart from anything that is unwholesome or unpleasing to you and make me a wife worthy of my spouse.

Amen

HEALTH
(HIS)

1 Corinthians 10:31

Notes

Dear Heavenly Father,

THANK YOU FOR GIVING ME the precious gift of an amazing husband. He is an incredible blessing to our family. He is a provider, a spiritual leader, a lover, a friend, a husband, a pilot. He lives and breathes for our family. He works long, hard hours and freely gives of himself to provide us with a great life. I know that all of his roles and responsibilities can be mentally, physically, and spiritually taxing. Sometimes he gets too tied up in the day-to-day frustrations and complicated politics of the aviation life and forgets to take proper care of himself. In addition, life on the road does not always offer the best solutions for a healthy lifestyle. He is often immobile for long periods of time, frequently does not get enough rest, and is forced to make poor food choices. Lord, I pray for my husband's physical, mental, and spiritual well-being. Help him to be more intentional about his own health. Please provide opportunities for him to get ample exercise and eat a healthy diet on the road as well as at home. Minimize the stress he experiences in all aspects of his life. Help him maintain a healthy mental status including adequate rest and daily quiet time with you. Teach him to actively seek the joy in each day and do not allow depression to have any foothold in his heart. Bless him with a long, happy, healthy life to spend loving his wife and, in turn, being loved by me too.

Amen

HEALTH
(MINE)

1 Corinthians 6:20

Notes

Dear Heavenly Father,

THERE ARE SO MANY THINGS that I love about being a pilot's wife. I love that I have a talented husband who works hard to provide for our family and that I get to be part of supporting his dreams. I love seeing my handsome man in his uniform...and out! I also enjoy my individualism and time alone to pursue my own hobbies and passions. However, oftentimes being the one who is left behind comes with its own share of frustrations and difficulties. Lord, you know that sometimes I feel lonely and overwhelmed when my husband is away for long periods of time. I often let the mundane, day-to-day chores take my focus off the things that matter most - you, my husband, my family, and my own health. In order to love a pilot, you must learn to F.L.Y. - to first love yourself. I know that I cannot take care of anyone else if I do not first take care of myself. I want to live a full life overflowing with joy, good health, and a happy marriage. Remove any guilt that weighs me down and keeps me from enjoying myself when he is away. Help me to refresh my mind and renew my soul regularly and focus on the things that truly matter most. My body is a temple. Remind me to eat healthy meals, seek preventative care, and get plenty of exercise and rest. Help me to fill my body with only healthy foods and my heart with only healthy advice. Remind me to spend quality time with you every day, Lord. I want to make healthy lifestyle choices for my body, mind, and soul because, when I love myself well, I can love my pilot and family well too.

Amen

OUR
MARRIAGE

Genesis 2:24

Notes

Dear Heavenly Father,

THANK YOU FOR THE BEAUTIFUL gift of our marriage. My husband is my confidante, my lover, and my best friend. I am grateful that you created us for one another - perfectly knit together from the womb to become husband and wife. I choose him, and he chooses me. Remind us daily why we fell in love and sustain our marriage. Teach each of us to be intentional about loving the other well, even when we are apart. Do not allow the physical distance between us to translate into an emotional distance. Instead, strengthen us and show us new and creative ways to solidify our emotional and physical bond. Help us to honor the vows that we took before you. Keep our feet firmly planted on the path of monogamy, never allowing us to stray from your beautiful and perfect plan for our marriage. I want to grow old beside my husband. Help us to love one another each and every day more than the last. Be our third, unbreakable strand, giving us fortitude on the days when love is hard and bringing us back to the core of hope that binds us together when we lose our way. Create within us a selfless love that defies circumstance, distance, or time. Fill us with compassion, understanding, gentleness, humility, forgiveness, patience, and endurance. He is my husband, and I am his wife. Our marriage is precious, beautiful, and worth fighting for. Help us to continue to choose one another every single day for the rest of our lives.

Amen

Notes

Dear Heavenly Father,

I ADMIT THAT I WILL never completely understand what my husband experiences while he is on the road and vice versa. I know that at times he faces loneliness, unexpected hurdles, temptation, and long days away from home and the arms of the people he loves. I know that he misses too many holidays and special occasions with our family and that he longs to be by my side during these moments as much as I long for him to be there. Help me to not laden him with guilt for those things which he cannot control but rather to see his difficult situation with clarity and show him the love and compassion he deserves. I also know that, though he loves to fly, he does not necessarily love the political aspects that accompany the job. Lord, I pray that you would surround my husband with encouragement. Let him know how incredible he is. Fill his life with people and circumstances that lift him up, bring him great joy, and encourage him along the way. Teach him to intentionally seek the beauty and joy in every single day, even on the hard ones. The world has more than its fair share of critics. Do not let me become another resounding gong in his life, but rather teach me to encourage him and love him in the ways that he needs to be loved. I want to be an amazing wife for my husband. He is my best friend and the biggest encourager in my life's journey. Let me be the biggest encourager in his life's journey too.

Amen

SKILL

Psalm 90:17

Notes

Dear Heavenly Father,

MY HUSBAND IS A BRILLIANT pilot. I have nothing but the utmost respect for his career. It takes an unfathomable amount of knowledge, skill, fortitude, and specialized training to do what he does. I am incredibly proud of his aviation and life accomplishments, and I hope he is too! Help me to voice my pride and respect openly to him. I pray that he continues to be teachable, learning and growing as the aviation field around him continues to change and advance. Give him ample opportunities for deserved promotion as well as stability in his current position. Lord, let him be well respected in his career and social circles, a role model for his co-workers, and a shining example for your kingdom in everything that he does. Help him to excel among his peers and give him unshakable confidence in his own abilities. Give him steady hands and sound decision-making when he is behind the yoke. I pray that you would also bring others into his path upon whom he can pass on his rich wealth of knowledge. When he faces stressful periods of recurrent training, give him the knowledge and composure that he needs to pass his exams with 'flying' colors. Hone and sharpen his skills continuously, creating in him the very best pilot that he can possibly be.

Amen

TIME
TOGETHER

Proverb 31:10-11

Notes

Dear Heavenly Father,

THANK YOU FOR LOVING ME so much that you hand created an amazing husband just for me. You knew exactly the type of man I needed to complete and compliment me, and you chose my wonderful pilot. Thank you for your foresight and wisdom in this perfect choice. He is my everything - my husband, my lover, my very best friend. Though the demands of the aviation life do not always afford us the ability to be together face-to-face, we are always together heart-to-heart. However, I pray that when we are able to be together, our time spent with one another is loving and joyful. Our moments together are more precious than jewels. Help us each put aside self for the sake of us. Fill our moments together with laughter, joy, and sweet memories. Do not let us linger in old hurts or harbor new anger, but instead allow apologies and forgiveness to flow freely between us. Help our moments together be rich and full of life. Draw us closer together every day and teach us to revel in our love for one another. Let us remember and constantly marvel about the fact that we were perfectly molded to be husband and wife by your flawless hand. In that knowing, let the moments of our years bind us together with beautiful memories and unconditional love for one another.

Amen

FORGIVENESS

Ephesians 4:32

Notes

Dear Heavenly Father,

MARRIAGE IS THE UNION OF two flawed, imperfect people striving to put aside their selfish tendencies for the sake of unity. Though my pilot and I try to love one another well, serve each other selflessly, and put the needs of the other above our own, we sometimes fall short. There have been times in our marriage when we have hurt one another, sometimes deeply. Though it's hard to let go of those hurts, unforgiveness is a rust that will slowly eat away at the framework of a marriage, destroying it from the inside out. I pray that you help my pilot and I to be generous forgivers. Help us to let go of all our past hurts. Teach us to be quick to offer forgiveness when we have been wronged and even quicker to offer apologies when we have done wrong. Lord, help us to treat each other with kindness, love, and respect in both word and deed, even when one of us feels slighted by the other. Teach us to set aside our foolish pride for the sake of marital unity. Help us forgive not only our past hurts, but also any that we will experience in the future. Give us a love for one another so deep that it resignates through time and surpasses all hurt and resentment. Afford us continuous forgiving spirits that keep our hearts pure and uncluttered with the baggage of life, that we might experience marriage the way it was truly meant to be.

Amen

HUMILITY

Ephesians 4:2

Notes

Dear Heavenly Father,

CONFIDENCE COMES FROM KNOWING THAT we are deeply loved by you and that you have gifted us with the passions and skills necessary to complete the good works you have laid out for us in advance. Pride, on the other hand, is a feeling of deep pleasure or satisfaction derived from one's own achievements for the purpose of gaining admiration from others in the world around us. It is no secret that you have gifted my husband with many incredible skills. He is an exceptional pilot. I am very proud of the man he is and extremely grateful that you have chosen him to be my life's partner. However, I pray that you instill a great sense of humility within him. Lord, let him constantly choose to lay down his pride for the sake of your greater plan. Remind him daily that all good gifts are from you and that you are the reason for all good gifts. Help him to always act in a kind, gentle way toward me and others. Do not allow arrogance to dwell in his heart, but rather create within him a vessel of genuine compassion for those he encounters daily. I want for him to be a confident man but not a prideful one. Give him the wisdom to discern between the two. Teach him to be last in this world so that he can be first in your kingdom and create within him a humble heart and gentle soul. Continue to sanctify and mold him into the man you desire him to be, constantly reminding him to humbly seek your will in all things.

Amen

CONTENTMENT
(HIS)

Philippians 4:12-13

Notes

Dear Heavenly Father,

I ADORE MY AVIATION HUSBAND. I know that he works exceedingly hard to provide a great life for us, and I could not be prouder of the extraordinary man that he is. I understand that the long hours, lonely nights, missed holidays, and complex aviation politics which come with the job can be difficult at times for him to endure. It can become understanably easy for him to become discouraged or even depressed and continually look to the next paycheck, the next schedule, the next upgrade, or the next airline for his happiness and contentment. However, true contentment is not found in the temporary, finite things of this world but rather in your infinite, unchanging love. When we spend all of our time focused on our trials and tribulations, we do not have time left to marvel at our many blessings. Teach him to marvel, Lord. Help him to look for and find contentment in the breathtaking horizons of each and every day. Let him seek his joy not in the disipating mists of an unpromised tomorrow but in the solid arms of the present. Help him focus on the things in his life he has instead of those things he lacks. Teach him to turn his eyes fully upon you for all of his happiness and not upon the temporary things this broken world has to offer. Fill my husband with unending peace and unrivaled contentment, not in the empty promises of tomorrow, but in the precious moments of today.

Amen

CONTENTMENT
(MINE)

Luke 12:15

Notes

Dear Heavenly Father,

I LOVE BEING A PILOT'S wife. You have provided me with an amazing life and an even more amazing husband. Thank you for your provision of a home, a vehicle, a family, food on our table, and people to encourage me along the journey. Forgive me, Lord, for the times when I take my eyes off the great blessings in my life and allow myself to focus instead on the things which I don't have. Help me to seek contentment and joy in the moments of each day. Turn my eyes from my selfish wants and place them instead upon my infinite blessings. Remind me each and every day that you have provided so much beauty in my life. I know that contentment is not found in acquiring more things but rather in being grateful for the current circumstances of my life. Lord, I know that the sky is not bluer on the other side. If I cannot find joy in today, then the next upgrade, job, or city will not fulfill the empty places in my heart. Teach me to find contentment in the now. Remind me that each and every breath that fills my lungs is a priceless gift from you. Do not allow me to continually place my hopes in material things but rather find joy in the beautiful moments of my life. Open my eyes, Lord, to the infinite blessings that surround me and change my heart to one that delights in every breath that you allow me to take, every moment that you allow me to spend with my husband, and every day that you choose to give me life.

Amen

Notes

Dear Heavenly Father,

MY HUSBAND SPENDS A LOT of time on the road, sleeping in different cities every night, working with a brand new crew every trip, meeting an endless array of passengers every day. He essentially spends a large portion of his life surrounded by complete strangers! I know these circumstances can often make it very difficult for him to initiate and sustain healthy, meaningful relationships. However, I also know how important it is to have foundational relationships to lean on for encouragement and support. I pray that you help him to spend quality time with those closest to him - whether with me, siblings, children, or parents. Help him to experience the immense joy that those familial relationships bring. He also needs friendships in his life that are reciprocal. There are so many takers in this world and not nearly enough givers. With his limited time at home, it can be difficult to find and hone quality friendships. It often feels like my husband is always giving of himself to others with little return. I pray that you would bring friendships of reciprocity into his life. Surround him with strong, intentional, Godly men who seek him out, encourage him, and speak truth to him. Bring intentional people into his life who are understanding of the nuances of aviation life and check on his wellbeing when he is on the road, when he often needs it most. Lord, fill his life with people that love him well, pray for him regularly, and encourage him on his life's journey and in our marriage.

Amen

JEALOUSY

Proverb 14:30

Notes

Dear Heavenly Father,

ONE OF THE GREAT IRONIES of aviation marriage is that my pilot and I are oftentimes jealous of one another. I imagine him off on exciting adventures in romantic locales while I sit alone at home covered in drool and old Spaghetti-O's. He imagines me laughing with our children and making memories on family picnics while he spends another lonely night clicking channels in a stark hotel room. We are experiencing the irrational fires of jealousy stoked by an invented reality and fueled by a lack of understanding for one another's situations. It is a volatile combination. Lord, be the buffer of my easily wandering heart. Rid me of any ill-conceived or hard feelings I may harbor toward him. Let me see the reality of his traveling life clearly that I might have a deep understanding of the trials he experiences. He is my beloved husband! I should be filled with great joy for the moments when he gets to experience beautiful things, even if I cannot be there. It's only natural that I miss him and desire to experience life with my husband. However, I deeply desire for him to have a rich and satisfying life, even we are apart. Lord, I pray that you replace any tendencies I have toward jealousy with tendencies toward compassion and grace. Forgive me for my moments of jealousy. Do not allow my natural tendencies to miss him turn into unnatural resentment. Fill me daily with tender love for my traveling spouse.

Amen

HIS
WORDS

Psalm 14:3

Notes

Dear Heavenly Father,

YOU CALL THE TONGUE A double-edged sword, and for good reason. We have within our mouths the tremendous power to build up or destroy another person. The words we choose to speak also pave the road our hearts will follow. I pray that you will fill my husband's mouth with words that are honoring to you and to our marriage. Teach him to speak only words that build up our marriage, our family, and those around him and convict his heart of those words that tear down and destroy. When he is away or online, do not let him fall into the easy trap of negative banter, but rather help him to immediately reject negativity. Give him a deep understanding of just how powerful his words can be and their ability to impact my heart as well as the hearts of others around him. Let him speak refreshing, gentle words of positivity that renew the spirit and refresh the soul. Help me always know I am cherished and loved by my husband through the words he chooses to speak. Help him to guard his tongue no matter who is within hearing range. In the same way, help me speak only uplifting and encouraging words to and about my spouse that build him up. Do not let me fall into the dangerous traps of gossip and negativity but rather lead my heart down the path of positivity that I might honor my husband as well.

Amen

LEADERSHIP

1 Corinthians 11:3

Notes

Dear Heavenly Father,

I KNOW THAT YOU CREATED men to be the head of the household. You have ingrained in them a deep desire to provide, protect, and lead. Many falsely portray this as a trait of dominance or inequality, but it is something far more pure of heart and infinitely more beautiful - the willingness to lay down his life because of his great love for me. A good man does not treat his wife as lesser but rather as more - as a precious and cherished gift. My husband longs to show me I am priceless by providing, protecting, and leading. My pilot is away from home often, however, and I must take control of the household in order for things to run smoothly while he is away. When he returns, I can often be overbearing and set in my ways, which makes him feel like he is not needed or does not fit into my life. I know this feeling can lead to hurt and resentment in him. I also know that sometimes I can feel hurt and resentful when he tries to take over the reins. Lord, this is not an easy transition for either of us, and we must navigate it several times each month. Help us to find a healthy balance in our home. Teach me to relinquish control to him when he returns and for him to feel needed and respected in his own home. Help me to understand that he is not trying to dominate or control me but rather to figure out how he fits in and to lead our home well despite our unusual circumstances. Help us to find ways to overcome the control struggle, being sensitive and compassionate to one another's feelings, slow to anger, and gentle in word and action.

Amen

BURDEN

Matthew 11:28

Notes

Dear Heavenly Father,

THE BURDEN ON THE SHOULDERS of a man is indeed great. He is the rock of the household, a provider, a leader, a protector, and a confidante to many. I know my pilot often feels the weight of his many roles, compounded by the fact that he cannot always be here when I need him most. I know how hard that can be for his heart to bear. We know that your yoke is light, Lord. I pray that you help him surrender all of his burdens to you. Teach him to trust you in the ultimate provision, protection, and leadership of our family. Likewise, help me to realize that my husband is an imperfect flesh-and-blood man. He does not have all the answers and cannot fill the gaps in my heart that were created to be filled only by you. Teach me to not place unreasonable demands on my husband that he cannot possibly fill. Remind me that he is my life's companion, not my savior. Help me to lean on you and surrender my own burdens daily. You came to give us abundant life. Teach my pilot to lay aside his burdens and accept your free gift. Free him from his daily worries so that he can experience the freedom of true joy. He is a wonderful man and the love of my life. I want him to be free of his burdens so that he can truly soar through this life!

Amen

IDENTITY

Jeremiah 1:5

Notes

Dear Heavenly Father,

MY HUSBAND IS AN EXTRAORDINARY man. Words cannot fully express how blessed I am to have the great honor of being called his wife. You created him, chose him, and specifically gifted him with the passions and skills to fly aircraft. I know that you gave these specific talents to him so that he might glorify you in all he does. It's so easy in our world for a man's identity to be largely defined by his career. However, he is much more than just a pilot. He is a husband, a son, a father, a friend. And Lord, most of all, he is yours. I also know that things in this world don't always go the way we plan and we sometimes face unexpected failures or big disappointments. These times can be very difficult on his heart. I pray that my husband seeks his identity and ultimate purpose not in his career, relationships, or the other temporary things of this world, but rather in the One who created and loves him unconditionally. Let my husband find his true identity only in you. I pray that you are the center of his life and the foundation for all of his decisions. Let him glorify you both on the good days and the bad. Do not let him be shaken by the uncontrollable circumstances of this life, but rather stand firmly upon the rock of your unchanging love. He is a priceless jewel in your holy crown. Let him be strong in you and bold for you. Help him to see how fiercely loved, beautifully created, and infinitely precious he is in your eyes.

Amen

SEXUAL
PURITY

Matthew 5:27-28

Notes

Dear Heavenly Father,

MY HUSBAND IS A KIND, wonderful, attractive man. I understand that he was created as a sensual being with sexual desires. It is hard for me to fully understand the important role that sexual intimacy fulfills in my husband's emotional wellbeing. However, it is enough for me to know that it is true. We live in a highly sexualized world filled with temptation. Aviation is a career of ample opportunity and limited accountability. Lord, I pray for the sexual purity of my husband. Help him reject temptation and keep his eyes and heart pure for me. Convict him of any sexual sin that has power in his life and give him the strength to overcome it. Do not let him be drawn into the sins of pornography, strip clubs, other businesses of sexual nature, prostitution, or infidelity. If he has sinned against our marriage in any of these ways, I pray that you would convict his heart to confession and repentance. If he has hurt me in this way, I pray for healing of my broken heart and the strength and wisdom I need to make my choices and carry on. Pair my pilot with men and women who respect the boundaries of their marriages and ours. Send him godly men to keep him accountable and speak truth into his life. Help me to have an open, gentle heart when discussing the temptations of the road with him so that I can better support him in his journey of sexual purity. Give us the courage to speak candidly about this very difficult reality of the aviation lifestyle and the wisdom to listen and speak with grace. Help him to remain faithful to our vows and pure of body and heart.

Amen

BEAUTY

1 Peter 3:3-4

Notes

Dear Heavenly Father,

I DO NOT ALWAYS RECOGNIZE my own beauty and value. The world judges beauty by our outward appearance, while you look to the content of our hearts. You have lovingly and perfectly created me by the work of your own skillful hand to fulfill a unique and specific purpose that only I can. Do not allow me to become discouraged and disillusioned by the shallow images of airbrushed femininity that constantly bombard me. Those images are unobtainable, unrealistic representations of true beauty. My husband thinks I am already beautiful! Do not let me long to become something I am not, but rather help me love the perfect, beautiful woman I see gazing back at me when I look in the mirror. I want to love myself fully so that I can fully give myself to my husband. I pray that you will help me see just how beautiful and incredible I truly am - just the way you created me to be. I am fearfully and wonderfully made! Teach me to be unapologetic about loving myself because I am worth it. I am more than enough, just the way that I am! I will not spend my life in a state of discontentment fueled by the superficiality of worldly beauty, but rather will embrace the beautiful woman that I already am. Do not allow me to seek my value through comparison to others but rather in your endless and perfect love for me. Help me to stand confidently upon my infinite self-worth and know without doubt that I am a beautiful, priceless treasure to you and to my spouse.

Amen

COMMUNITY

Titus 3:10

Notes

Dear Heavenly Father,

I AM GRATEFUL FOR THE amazing career with which you have gifted my husband. I am very proud of him for pursuing his dreams and for the great success he has experienced in his chosen field. However, it is also a field heavily swathed in a culture of negativity. There are many people who seek to focus on the nuances and problems of aviation life instead of the joys and successes, complaining loudly to anyone that will listen about their bitter discontentment. I pray that you will help my pilot and I both seek and find community that encourages us in our journey through this life. Surround us with those who pour positivity and support into our lives and marriage, lifting us up and helping us to seek joy and reconciliation in all circumstances. When negativity tries to gain a foothold in our lives, give us the wisdom to quickly recognize it for what it is and the strength to immediately reject it. Lord, I know that what we pour into our hearts will eventually pour back out in deed and word. Send us people that fill us with hope, encouragement, and joy so that the overflow of our hearts is pure and full of life and love. Let us not harbor negativity for even a moment, instead directing our hearts, eyes, and minds only to those things, people, and communities that will hasten us upon our life's journey with exceeding joy and never-ending hope. Help me to be a wife worthy of my husband's praise and vice versa, creating between us a marriage that is a bright and shining star of hope and positivity in this community for others to follow.

Amen

REST

Psalm 23:1-2

Notes

Dear Heavenly Father,

LORD, THANK YOU FOR PROVIDING me with an amazing, hardworking husband who always puts me first in his life. I know that he chooses to work hard for the benefit of our family. Thank you for his willingness to provide for our family and the way he works tirelessly to make sure that we are well loved and well cared for. My husband is an incredible man with a beautiful heart and kind spirit. I also know that the burdens of his career, family, and the world sometimes weigh heavily on his tired shoulders. Even the strongest men need to take time to rest their bodies and refresh their spirits every now and then. I pray that my husband finds time to rest. Help him to get ample sleep and provide him with plenty of chances to replenish both physically as well as spiritually. As you demonstrated to us on the seventh day, rest is an important part of your perfect, beautiful plan for our lives. Help him to take time from his busy schedule to renew himself. Remove any guilt that might be barring his ability to rest. Do not allow me to become resentful when he has downtime but rather thankful that the man I love has an opportunity to rejuvenate his soul. In the same way, remind me how important it is for me to rest and replenish myself as well. Help me to take time to relax and unwind. I know how important rest is for our souls and ultimately for our marriage. Lord, help us both to rest easy in you.

Amen

INTIMACY

Mark 10:7-8

Notes

Dear Heavenly Father,

MY HUSBAND IS A SENSUAL being created with sexual needs and desires. These are not bad qualities but rather beautiful gifts given by you to be used within the confines of marriage. A woman's perception of sexuality can often vary greatly from that of a man's. I understand that sexuality is very closely tied to a man's emotional experiences of love and acceptance and that he desperately needs to be pursued and desired by his wife. I want to fulfill my husband in this important way, and I know how essential a satisfying sex life is for a good marriage. However, sometimes our chaotic schedules, his long stints away from home, and our different libidos can make intimacy challenging. Lord, place in me a deep desire for my husband. Help me to be open to his advances. Teach me to overcome whatever body image issues I harbor and pursue my husband without inhibition. Help me see sexuality not as something dirty or embarrassing but rather as the beautiful gift you meant it to be. Remove any pain that I experience during intercourse so that I can experience intimacy with my husband in a rich, satisfying way. Teach my husband to be patient as I learn to open myself up to him and gentle as we explore a new level of intimacy. Help us create a safe environment in our bedroom that gives us confidence to explore and learn without judgement or embarrassment. Deepen our love for one another and strengthen our relationship through satisfying sexual intimacy, solidifying our inseparable bond as husband and wife.

Amen

OUR
FUTURE

Mark 10:9

Notes

Dear Heavenly Father,

ONCE UPON A TIME, I stood upon an altar and chose my husband, and he chose me. On that beautiful day, we became husband and wife. He was the love of my life, and I was his one and only. On that day, we stood hand-in-hand on the brink of the rest of our lives staring forever boldly in the eyes. The future was ours to conquer. Over the years, through laughter and tears, we have continued to choose one another. Today, I pray for our tomorrows. Let us lock fingers with white-knuckled tenacity and refuse to let go because our marriage is worth fighting for. Sometimes it will be easy; sometimes it will be difficult. However, the choice is always ours to make. My husband is not the enemy; he is the man I fell in love with. He is not expendable; he is the man I vowed my heart to. We stood on that altar and promised to cherish each other for the rest of our lives. Lord, let it be so! I pray that we will have a future filled with tremendous joy, incredible memories, and endless laughter. Do not allow the physical distance to steal away our love, but rather let it strengthen our resolve. Help us love one another so fiercely that the rest of the world stands up and takes notice. Let us refuse to let go, always choosing one another. And at the end of the runway of life, let us be found still standing hand-in-hand and more in love than the day we stood at the altar and said, 'I do.'.

Amen

About the Author

ANGELIA GRIFFIN IS A TALENTED four-time published author and mainstream blogger. Her works include The Crystal Keys series: Champion of Destiny and Sera Oth Berinon which she penned with her late mentor and Uncle, Gary Follis. She is also the CEO of AGF Publishing and the author of The Pilot Wife Life (thepilotwifelife.com) and My Best Laid Plans (angeliagriffin.com).

The Pilot Wife Life is a community created to pour encouragement and support into the aviation community in an effort to strengthen aviation marriages. Angelia is a pilot's wife who decided to make a difference. Her following continues to grow as she explores new and innovative ways to change the culture of aviation from the inside out with an outpouring of positivity and support.

Angelia and her husband live on a quaint homestead in the greater Houston area where they home school their two beautiful children. They are liaisons for a local homeless ministry and are heavily involved in many others, tirelessly volunteering within their community whenever and wherever they are needed.

To My Husband...

FOLD ALONG LINE

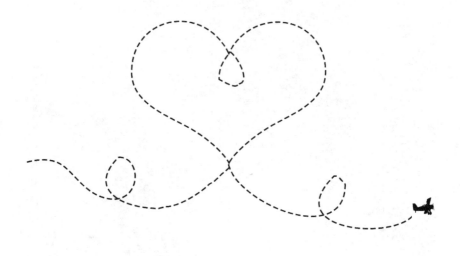

You are the man I fell in love with, my best friend, my lover. You are deeply loved, desired, and respected by your wife. Our marriage is worth fighting for, that's why I want you to know I am starting a new intentional prayer journey for you and our marriage.

I love you, my husband - yesterday, today, and always.